Exam MA1

Management Information

Pocket Notes

British library cataloguing-in-publication data

A catalogue record for this book is available from the British Library.

Published by:
Kaplan Publishing UK
Unit 2 The Business Centre
Molly Millars Lane
Wokingham
Berkshire
RG41 2QZ

ISBN 978-1-78740-424-3

Printed and bound in Great Britain.

Contents

Preface

These Pocket Notes contain everything you need to know for the exam, presented in a unique visual way that makes revision easy and effective.

Written by experienced lecturers and authors, these Pocket Notes break down content into manageable chunks to maximise your concentration.

Quality and accuracy are of the utmost importance to us so if you spot an error in any of our products, please send an email to mykaplanreporting@kaplan.com with full details, or follow the link to the feedback form in MyKaplan.

Our Quality Co-ordinator will work with our technical team to verify the error and take action to ensure it is corrected in future editions.

Introduction

In this chapter

- Overview of the examination.
- Keys to success.

Overview of the examination

This examination consists of 50 multiple choice questions – the examination itself lasts two hours. Computer based options are available.

Overview of the syllabus

- The nature and purpose of Cost and management accounting
- Source documents and coding
- Cost classification and measurement
- Recording costs
- Providing Information
- The spreadsheet system

Keys to success

As the examination is multiple choice only, you do need to consider the following:

- Multiple choice questions allow the examiner to cover a significant amount of the syllabus within each examination. This means you cannot simply learn say 50% of the syllabus and hope to achieve a pass standard – you will need to learn the entire syllabus to maximise your chances of passing.

- Questions are a mix of theory and practical. Be prepared to have to make appropriate calculations to find an answer – and always check that your answer is reasonable before marking your solution, e.g. an adverse variance of $30,000 is unlikely to be correct when total expenditure is only $20,000.

- Your question practice must be focused on multiple choice questions. As part of your revision, work through the questions in the Study Text and any question banks you may have to ensure you understand the style of question asked.

- Remember in the examination, you can answer questions in any order (as long as you complete the multiple choice boxes on the Candidate Registration Sheet correctly). It is therefore worth completing the easier questions first and then re-visit the more difficult questions at the end of the examination. This approach will (hopefully) ensure you have obtained the easy marks if you run out of time.

Finally, when all else fails – guess – there is no negative marking.

chapter

1

Business organisation

In this chapter

- The office.
- Double-entry bookkeeping.
- Computerised accounting systems.

The office

Definition

Office: an area/room providing administration functions for a company.

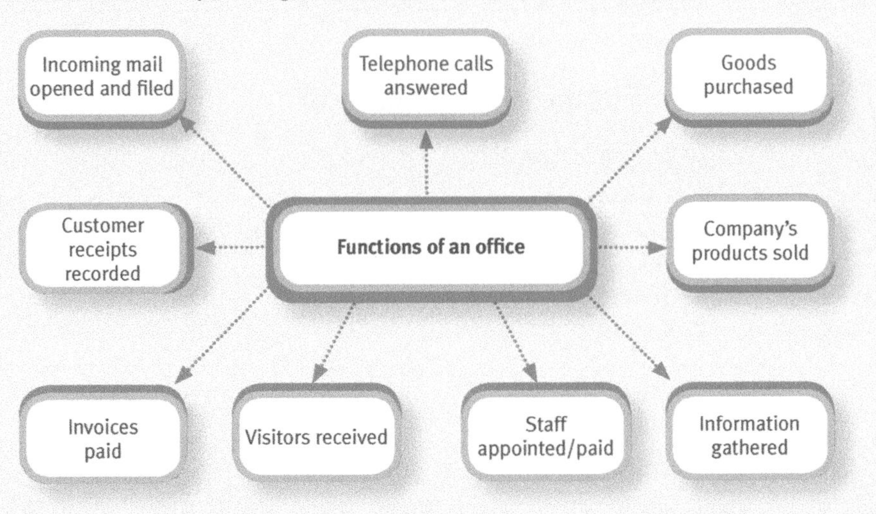

Offices can be:

- Centralised = all office procedures carried out at one central point.
- Decentralised = each department has their own office.

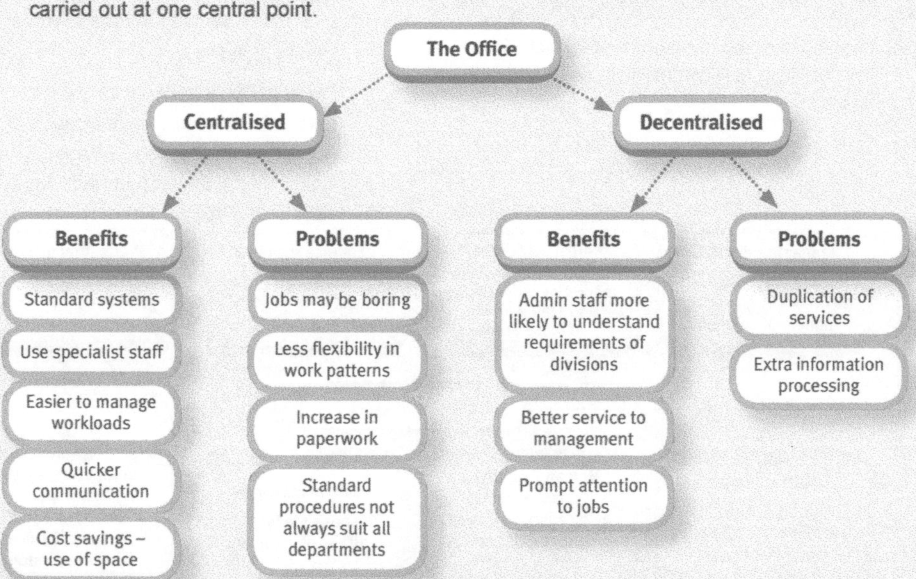

Offices have an organisation chart.

Definition

Organisation chart: diagram of formal relationships and communication flows in office.

Organisation chart shows:

- Names of individuals and their roles
- Line structure (who reports to whom)
- Levels of authority
- Supervisory structure
- Lines of essential communication.

Each department in organisation has a manager running that department. Typical managers include:

Managing director
Co-ordinates work of all other managers and running of company

Marketing manager
Responsible for sales, marketing, advertising and staff working in these areas

Finance manager
Responsible for financial and cost-accounting – has team of accounts staff

Production manager
Oversees production of goods and maintenance of production equipment

Office Managers

R&D manager
Manages design, development and testing of new products

Human Resources manager
Also called Personnel – manages all aspects relating to staff

Admin manager
Responsible for legal affairs of company

Computer services manager
Manager + staff responsible for all computer systems

Staff work in offices. Typical office layouts include:

Open plan	Large number of employees work together in one office. Easy to make changes to layout and provides good communication. Can be noisy.
Landscaped	Desks and furniture placed randomly to break up floor area and provide more 'natural' working environment.
Corridor offices	All offices lead off central corridor. Tend to be older buildings and does not promote communication and team working.

All offices have procedures = series of operations necessary to perform a given task.

Procedures will ensure:

- Smooth flow of work
- Minimal movement of staff
- Duplication of work avoided
- Make best use of specialist skills
- Provision of simple and easy-to-use systems
- Use of computers to support humans
- Systems in place are cost-effective.

Double-entry bookkeeping

Definition

Double-entry bookkeeping: a method of recording accounting transactions in books of company.

Computerised accounting systems

Computerised accounting systems = maintaining accounts on computer.

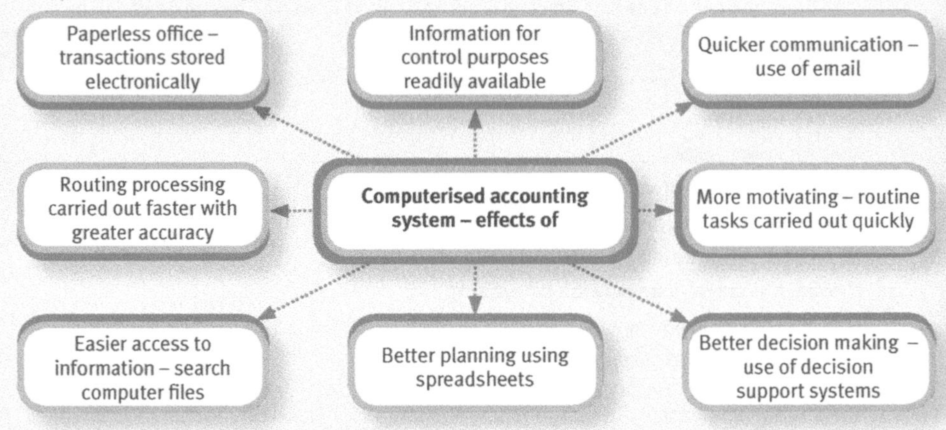

Methods of processing transactions:

Batch processing	Real time processing
• = Transactions collected and stored then processed in one large batch. • Provides good control of processing but accounts never up-to-date.	• = Transactions input and processed as they occur. • Means accounts always up-to-date but needs more staff and has more security issues.

Many computer systems are integrated i.e. all relevant accounts updated for each transaction e.g. payment to supplier updates bank, supplier's individual account and Purchase Ledger Control Account.

An alternative to integrated accounts is interlocking accounts where:

- Cost accounts are distinct from financial accounts.
- Two sets of accounts are 'interlocked' by use of control accounts.

Advantages of integrated systems include:

- Data only entered once.
- Less likelihood of human error – because data input once only.
- Information more accurate – because systems integrated.

Exam focus

Many examination questions focus on responsibilities in a company and the format of an office. These are therefore important areas for revision.

chapter

2

Introduction to management information

In this chapter

- Management information.
- Sources and categories of information.
- Comparison of management accounting and financial accounting.
- Management accounting versus financial accounting.
- Responsibility centres.
- Cost units.

Management information

Definition

Management information needed for decision making.

Types of decision:

Long-term decisions	Short-term decisions
• Concern future direction of business • Relate to products manufactured, how many staff to employ, purchase of machinery, etc	• About day-to-day running of business • Relate to scheduling of production, overtime requirements and amount of inventory to hold

Information terms

- Data = raw facts prior to processing
- Information = processed data – data in useful form
- Informed decisions = decision making based on appropriate, available information

Information also used for:

- Planning – strategic direction of business and the production of budgets
- Control – reviewing whether budgets achieved and taking remedial action

Features of quality information

Feature	Explanation	Problem
Relevant	Relate to needs of users	Users have different information requirements
Reliable	Can be trusted	Difficult – complex systems may make info unreliable
Understandable	No jargon	Different users have different levels of ability
Complete	All information available	User does not want too much information
Accurate	As error free as possible	Difficult to determine level of accuracy
Timely	Not late	Short production time scales may cause errors
Clear	Easily understood	Different abilities of different users
Consistent	Produced using consistent principles	May introduce element of rigidity to reporting process
Cost effective	Cost of production not exceed benefits of use	Difficult to determine benefits prior to use

Sources and categories of information

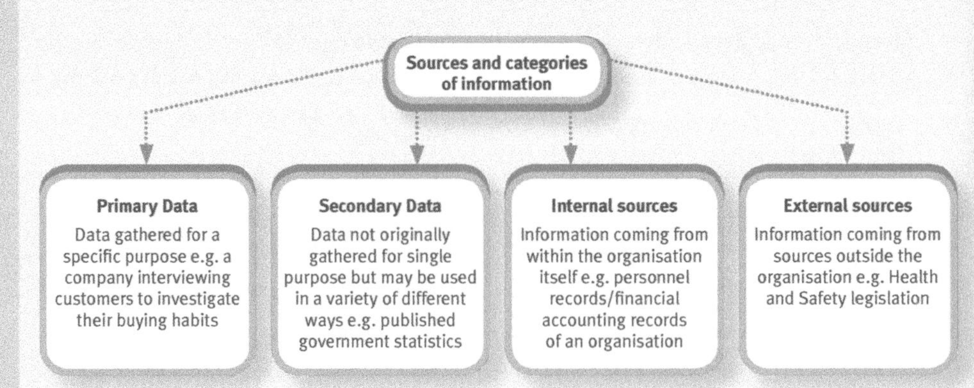

Comparison of management accounting and financial accounting

Types of accounting system

Financial accounting	Cost accounting	Management accounting
• = the classification and recording of monetary transactions • Presenting transactions to assess business performance • Typical accounts = income statement and balance sheet	• = establishing budgets and standard costs to control production activities • Very detailed outputs • Typically include variance analysis reports	• = identifying, presenting and interpreting information on strategic direction of company • Strategic output • Typically include financial and cost accounting information

Management accounting versus financial accounting

Feature	Financial accounting	Management accounting
Legal requirement	• Limited companies must produce financial accounts	• No requirement
Cost	• Necessity	• Must be justified
Objectives	• Satisfy Companies Act requirements	• Satisfy management
Time orientation	• Historical	• Historical to future
Content	• Satisfy Companies Act requirements	• To include information management requests
Reporting focus	• External	• Internal

Responsibility centres

Definition

Responsibility centre: part of organisation for which performance can be measured and is controlled by specific manager.

Exam focus

There are many definitions and facts in this section. You need to learn these to answer the exam style question of completing definitions.

Three types of responsibility centre

Cost centre	Profit centre	Investment centre
• = production or service location for which costs can be determined • May include stores, production department, canteen, etc	• = production or service location for which costs, revenues and therefore profit can be determined • Likely to refer to division or separate location of company • Revenue determination important to check performance of location	• = production or service location for which costs, revenues and net assets can be determined • Therefore a profit centre plus determines use of assets and liabilities • Performance measured by calculating ROCE or RI (see later)

Cost units

Definition

Cost unit: a unit of product or service in relation to which costs are ascertained, i.e. it is the basic unit of output of the business.

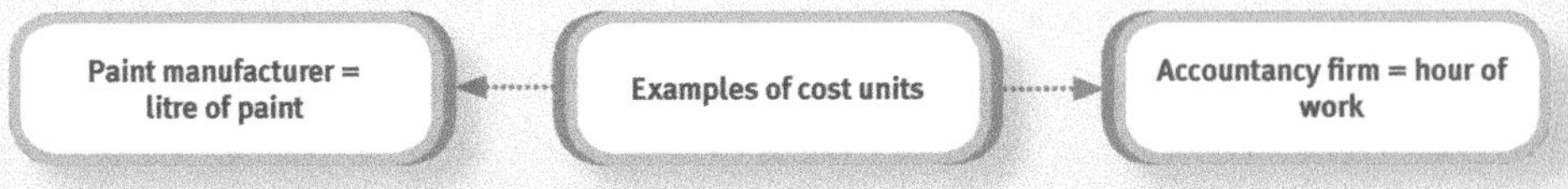

Importance of ascertaining cost per cost unit:

- making decisions about pricing
- measuring changes in costs as activity level changes
- inventory valuation
- planning future costs
- controlling costs.

Key Point

Composite cost units are made up of two parts and are often used in service organisations.

For example a haulage firm could use cost per tonne mile.

chapter

3

Classification of costs and cost behaviour

In this chapter

- Cost classification.
- Cost behaviour patterns.
- Direct costs and indirect costs.

Cost classification

Methods of classifying costs

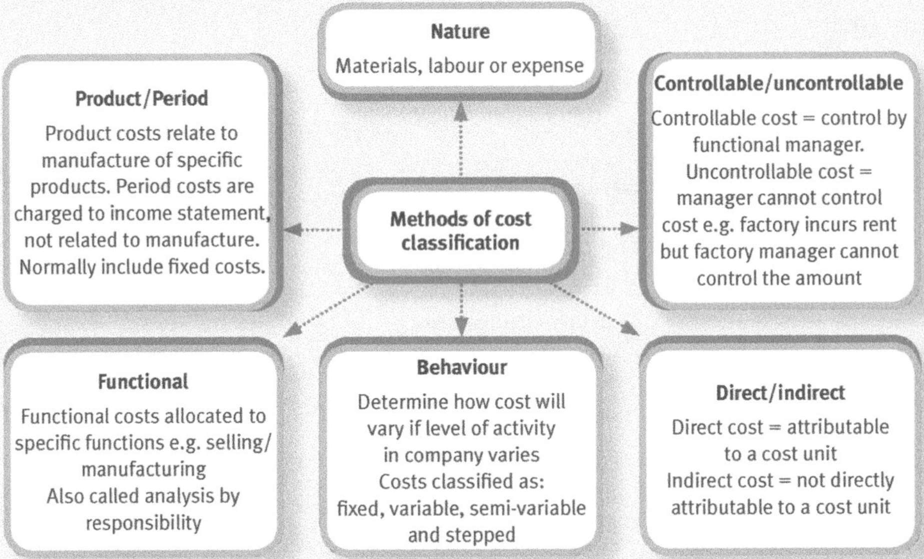

Methods of cost classification

Nature

Materials, labour or expense

Product/Period

Product costs relate to manufacture of specific products. Period costs are charged to income statement, not related to manufacture. Normally include fixed costs.

Controllable/uncontrollable

Controllable cost = control by functional manager.
Uncontrollable cost = manager cannot control cost e.g. factory incurs rent but factory manager cannot control the amount

Functional

Functional costs allocated to specific functions e.g. selling/ manufacturing
Also called analysis by responsibility

Behaviour

Determine how cost will vary if level of activity in company varies
Costs classified as: fixed, variable, semi-variable and stepped

Direct/indirect

Direct cost = attributable to a cost unit
Indirect cost = not directly attributable to a cost unit

Cost behaviour patterns

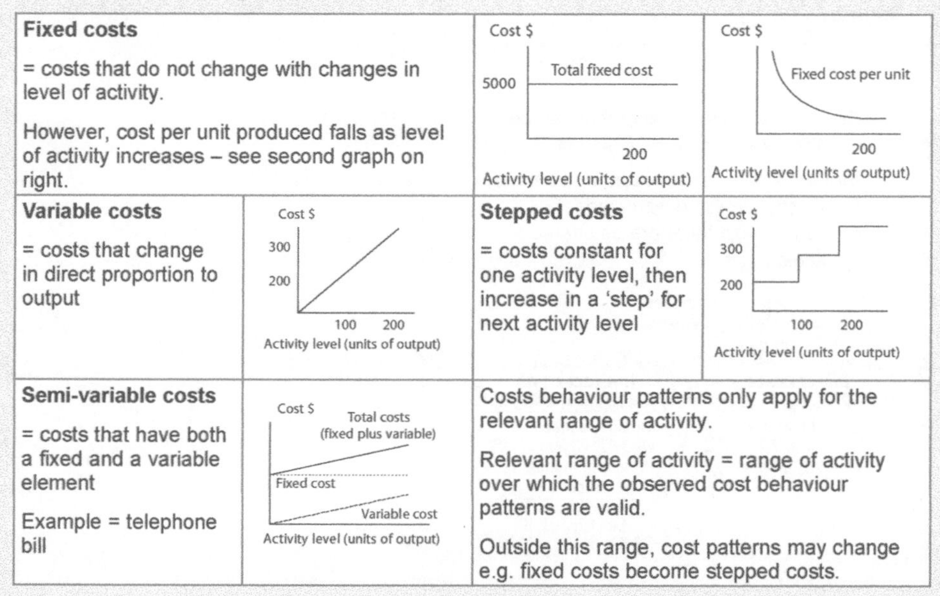

Direct costs and indirect costs

Definition

- **Direct costs:** expenditure that can be identified with a specific cost unit.
- **Indirect costs:** expenditure that cannot be directly identified with a specific cost unit. Must therefore be shared on equitable basis.

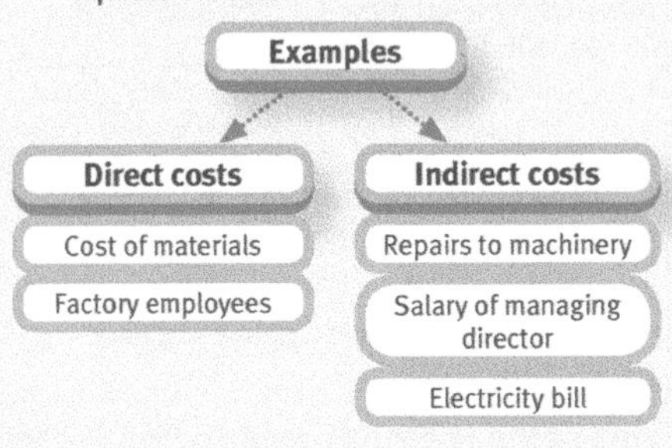

chapter

4

Coding of costs and income

In this chapter

- Coding of costs.

Coding of costs

Definition

Cost code: reference applied to a set of items, to give an accurate reference for collation and analysis of those items

- Need because items need to be allocated to cost centres for analysis purposes.
- Cost codes enable this analysis to be performed.

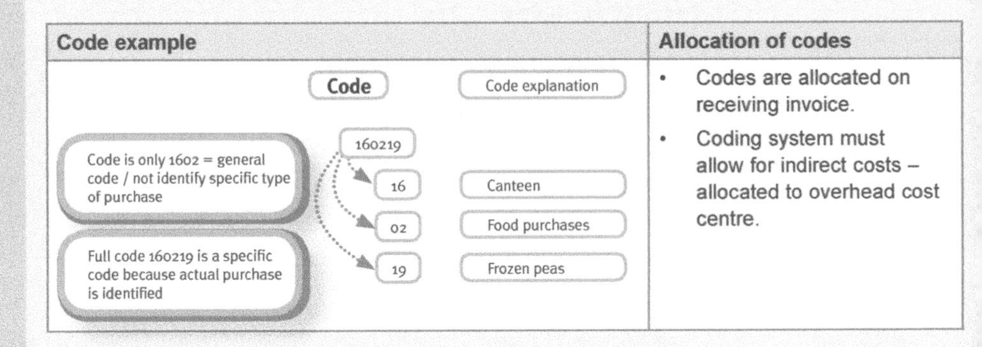

Allocation of codes

- Codes are allocated on receiving invoice.
- Coding system must allow for indirect costs – allocated to overhead cost centre.

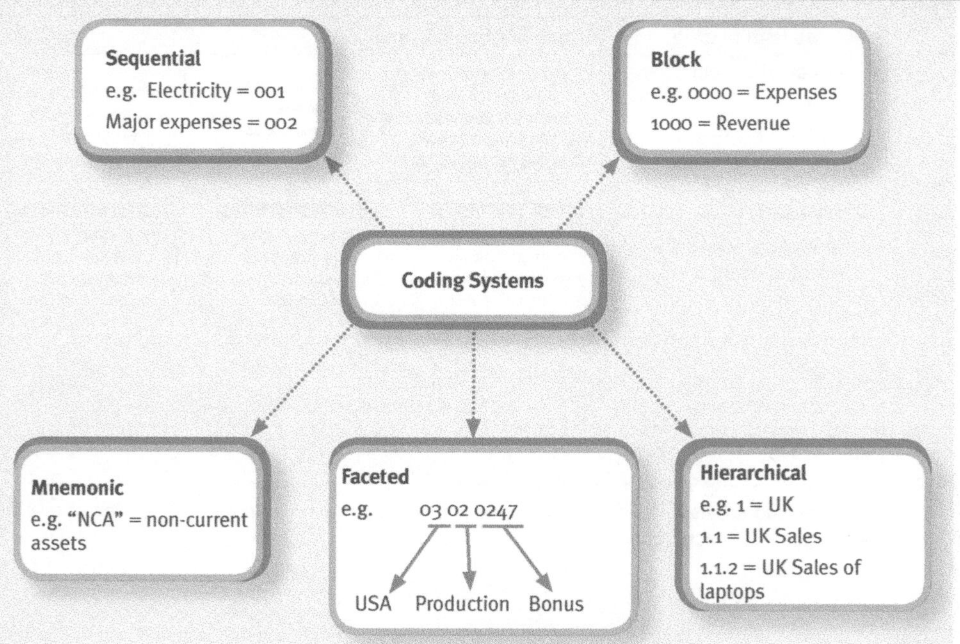
Sequential
e.g. Electricity = 001
Major expenses = 002
Block
e.g. 0000 = Expenses
1000 = Revenue
Coding Systems
Mnemonic
e.g. "NCA" = non-current assets
Faceted
e.g. 03 02 0247
USA
Production
Bonus
Hierarchical
e.g. 1 = UK
1.1 = UK Sales
1.1.2 = UK Sales of laptops

Problems with coding	Purposes of cost codes
• Allocating correct code to item • Apportioning cost over more than one cost centre (where necessary) • Correcting incorrectly allocated items	

Exam focus

Check that you are happy with the definitions in this section and can provide examples of relevant costs or items for each definition.

chapter

5

Materials cost

In this chapter

- Materials cost classification.
- Types of inventory.
- Purchasing and storage of materials.
- Recording of inventory.
- Materials ordering system.
- Monitoring inventory levels.
- Pricing issues of materials.

Materials cost classification

Definition

Direct materials: materials that can be economically attributed to a specific unit of production.

Direct materials = raw materials directly input into products made e.g. flour used to make bread

Definition

Indirect materials: other materials used in production process that cannot be directly attributed to a specific unit of production.

Indirect materials = general materials used in production e.g. oil used for lubrication of production machinery

Types of inventory

- Raw materials
- Work in progress
- Finished goods

Purchasing and storage of materials

Functions of stores department	Controls of purchasing – controls required
• Receipt of goods – check to purchase order to ensure correct goods delivered • Storage of materials – until required under correct conditions • Issue of materials – to production departments • Recording of receipts and issues – on bin cards or computer inventory system	• Only necessary items are purchased • Orders placed with most appropriate supplier (cost and quality considerations) • Goods received = goods actually ordered • Price charged for goods = price on price list

Recording of inventory

Two main systems:

1 Bin card = Record of receipts, issues and balance for each inventory line.

2 Materials ledger account = records the quantity and value of receipts, issues and balance for each inventory line.

Materials ordering system

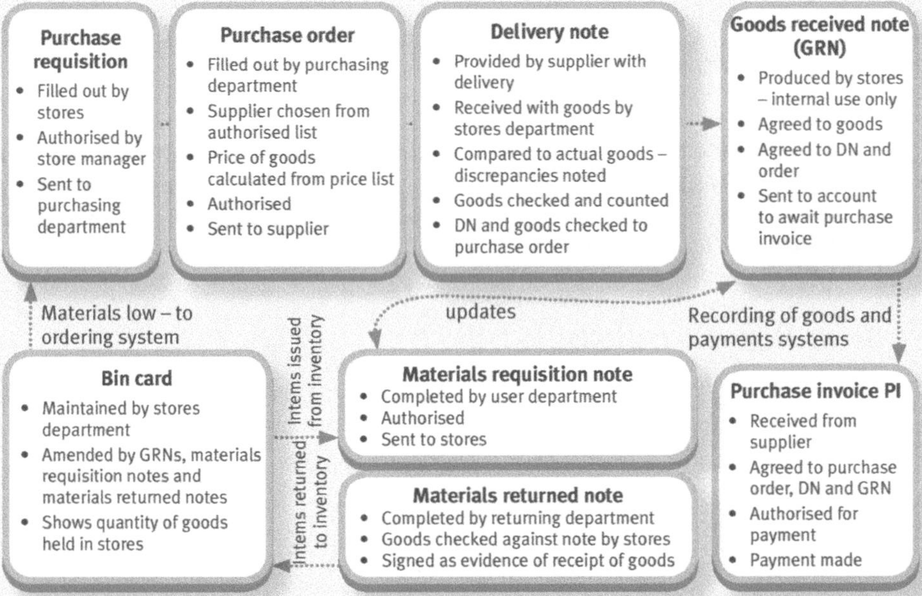

Purchase requisition
- Filled out by stores
- Authorised by store manager
- Sent to purchasing department

Purchase order
- Filled out by purchasing department
- Supplier chosen from authorised list
- Price of goods calculated from price list
- Authorised
- Sent to supplier

Delivery note
- Provided by supplier with delivery
- Received with goods by stores department
- Compared to actual goods – discrepancies noted
- Goods checked and counted
- DN and goods checked to purchase order

Goods received note (GRN)
- Produced by stores – internal use only
- Agreed to goods
- Agreed to DN and order
- Sent to account to await purchase invoice

Materials low – to ordering system

Intems issued from inventory

updates

Recording of goods and payments systems

Bin card
- Maintained by stores department
- Amended by GRNs, materials requisition notes and materials returned notes
- Shows quantity of goods held in stores

Intems returned to inventory

Materials requisition note
- Completed by user department
- Authorised
- Sent to stores

Materials returned note
- Completed by returning department
- Goods checked against note by stores
- Signed as evidence of receipt of goods

Purchase invoice PI
- Received from supplier
- Agreed to purchase order, DN and GRN
- Authorised for payment
- Payment made

Monitoring inventory levels

Need to ensure inventory levels are 'optimum', e.g.

- Not too high to incur high storage costs
- Not too low to cause stockouts.

Use free inventory to monitor inventory levels

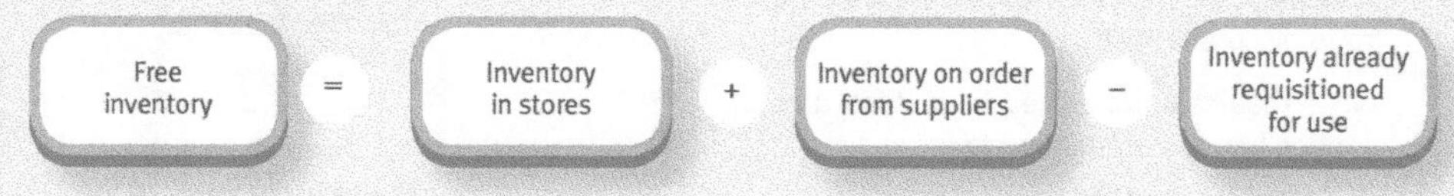

Exam focus

There are many different documents involved in the materials systems. Check you are happy with the purpose of each document.

Pricing issues of materials

When materials are purchased, the process of giving them a value is fairly straightforward. The purchase cost of the items is the price charged by the supplier (excluding any Sales tax) plus any carriage inwards costs. The cost should be net of any trade discount given.

When materials are issued from store, a cost or price has to be attached to them.

- When a quantity of materials is purchased in its entirety for a specific job, the purchase cost can be charged directly to the job.
- More commonly however, materials are purchased in fairly large quantities (but at different prices each time) and later issued to cost centres in smaller quantities. This requires an assumption about which order the goods are used in, so that each issue can be priced correctly.

Inventory valuation methods

FIFO – first in first out
Assume oldest inventory is used first

LIFO – last in first out
Assume newest inventory is used first

AVCO – weighted average cost
Assume inventory is combined and a new price is calculated each time there is a new delivery

Periodic weighted average cost
Calculate average price at end of relevant period

e.g

Example

There was no inventory of materials on hand at the start of the month. 50 tonnes was purchased on the 2nd of the month for $40 per tonne and a further 40 tonnes was purchased on the 10th for $45 per tonne. On the 15th a consignment of 30 tonnes was taken and used in the manufacturing process.

- **First in first out (FIFO)**

  Assume that the oldest inventory is used first: Issue of 30 tonnes priced at $40 per tonne.

- **Last in first out (LIFO)**

  Assume that the newest inventory is used first: Issue of 30 tonnes priced at $45 per tonne.

- **Weighted average cost (AVCO).**

  Assume that the inventory is combined and each unit is priced at the average cost of inventory on hand:

  (50 tonnes at $40) + (40 tonnes at $45) = 90 tonnes costing $3,800 = $42.22 per tonne.

  Issue of 30 tonnes priced at $42.22 per tonne.

- **Periodic weighted average cost**

  With the periodic weighted average cost method of pricing inventory an average price is calculated at the end of the period which is then used to price all issues.

- **Periodic weighted average price =**

$$\frac{\text{Cost of opening inventory + Receipts in the period}}{\text{Units in opening inventory + Units received}}$$

Note that there is no need for the accounting assumption about the order in which inventory is consumed to bear any relation to the actual pattern of consumption.

A business can choose whichever method of inventory valuation it wants to use for costing purposes (although LIFO is not acceptable for external financial reporting).

If the purchase price of materials stayed the same indefinitely, every inventory valuation method would produce the same values for stores issues and closing inventory. Differences between the valuation methods is usually only significant during a period of price inflation, because the choice of valuation method can have a significant effect on the value of materials consumed (and so on the cost of sales and profits) and on closing inventory values.

The relative advantages and disadvantages of FIFO, LIFO and AVCO are therefore discussed below, particularly in relation to **inflationary situations.**

Method	Advantages	Disadvantages
FIFO	• Produces current values for closing inventory.	• Produces out-of-date production costs and therefore potentially overstates profits. • Complicates inventory records as inventory must be analysed by delivery.
LIFO	• Produces realistic production costs and therefore more realistic/ prudent profit figures.	• Produces unrealistically low closing inventory values. • Complicates inventory records as inventory must be analysed by delivery.
Weighted average price	• Simple to operate – calculations within the inventory records are minimised.	• Produces both inventory values and production costs which are likely to differ from current values.

Whichever method is adopted it should be applied consistently from period to period.

chapter

6

Labour costs

In this chapter

- Recording labour costs.
- Gross pay.
- Bonus schemes.
- Group bonus schemes.
- Payroll.
- Productivity.

Recording labour costs

Employee personnel records	Key wages terms
• Labour costs = record of each employee for employment purposes • Includes: • Record of attendance = hours actually at work • Holiday = number of days allowed each year • Sickness = company policy for and number of days taken • Other absence e.g. for training or unauthorised absence.	• Clock card = document which records starting and finishing time for each employee for each day's work • Time sheet = record of time at work – shows time spent on jobs not simply total time at work (latter is the clock card) • Idle time = hours when employee at work and being paid but no output achieved e.g. machine breakdowns • Job sheet = record of number and type of product produced by each employee.

Gross pay

Two types:

1 Time-related: employee paid fixed amount regardless of amount of production achieved.

2 Output-related: employee paid according to amount of output produced.

Time-related pay

Salaried employees

- = gross pay fixed at agreed amount for period of time irrespective of hours worked
- Minimum number of hours worked stated
- May obtain overtime payment – depends on contract

Hourly rate employees

- = paid set hourly rate for each hour worked
- Rate of pay set for each hour of attendance

Overtime

- = number of hours worked by employee which exceeds contracted hours to be worked
- Normally receive "overtime premium" = higher wage for additional hours worked

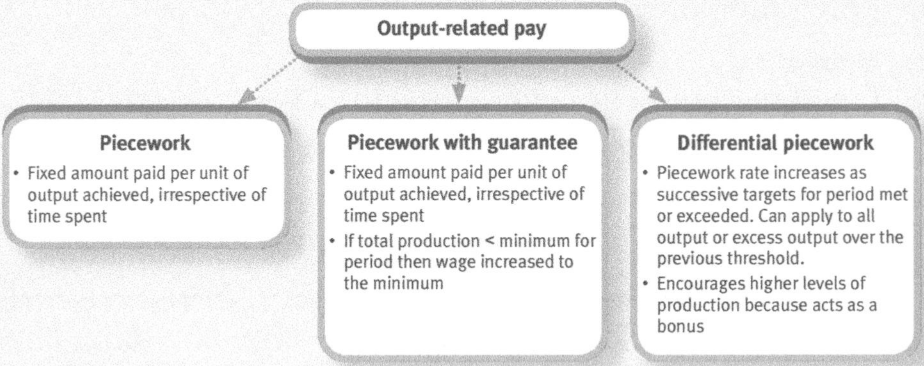

Output-related pay

Piecework

- Fixed amount paid per unit of output achieved, irrespective of time spent

Piecework with guarantee

- Fixed amount paid per unit of output achieved, irrespective of time spent
- If total production < minimum for period then wage increased to the minimum

Differential piecework

- Piecework rate increases as successive targets for period met or exceeded. Can apply to all output or excess output over the previous threshold.
- Encourages higher levels of production because acts as a bonus

Output-related pay:

Benefits	Problems
• No limit on how much employee can earn (if work hard) • Encourages higher output (good from employer point of view)	• Needs accurate recording of items produced (otherwise system open to potential fraud) • Needs close monitoring of quality of output (faster work may cause fall in quality of items produced)

Bonus schemes

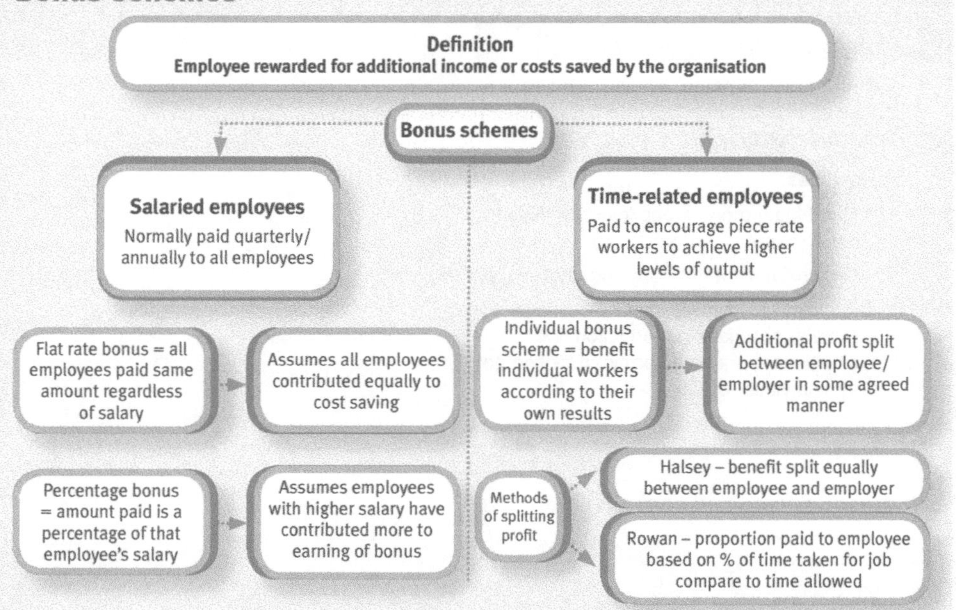

Group bonus schemes

Definition

Group bonus scheme: bonus based on output of workforce and shared between individual members of the group.

Advantages:

- May obtain more 'group loyalty' – fewer days absent.
- Easy to monitor – record output of group not the worker.
- More appropriate in production line situations – output determined by line not the individual worker.

Payroll

Manufacturing industry	Service industry
• Payroll costs include employer's NIC • Time and costs of payroll coded to relevant jobs • Service centre employees, time and costs coded against the relevant service centre	• Payroll costs include employer's NIC • No physical units produced • Labour costs relate to time work – allocated to jobs on this basis (e.g. accountancy firm)

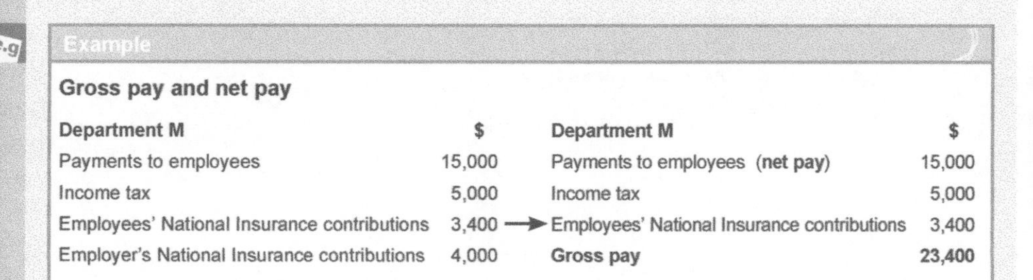

e.g

Example

Gross pay and net pay

Department M	**$**
Payments to employees	15,000
Income tax	5,000
Employees' National Insurance contributions	3,400
Employer's National Insurance contributions	4,000

→

Department M	**$**
Payments to employees (**net pay**)	15,000
Income tax	5,000
Employees' National Insurance contributions	3,400
Gross pay	**23,400**

Productivity

Definition

Productivity: the amount of output produced per labour hour.

- Employee paid on time basis then increased productivity means cost per unit falls (more units produced in given time)
- Employee paid on output related pay, then increased productivity means no change in cost per unit – costs already allocated against units produced

Exam focus

There are a lot of terms to remember in this chapter, so make sure that you have a good understanding of them. The difference between output related and time related pay is one of the key areas to understand from this chapter.

chapter

7

Expenses and absorption of overheads

In this chapter

- Expenses.
- Cost centres and expenses.
- Selling function.
- Methods of overhead absorption.

Expenses

Definition

Expenses: all business costs that are not classified as materials or labour costs.

- Few expenses are direct = royalty payments per unit of output.
- Most expenses are indirect = not associated with any production units.

Examples of expenses

Manufacturing	Selling	Administrative	Finance
Sub-contractors	Advertising	Rent of buildings	Loan interest
Factory light and heat	Delivery costs	Telephone bills	Lease charges
Machinery power	Sales reps' commission	Stationery	

	Capital	Revenue
Definition	Money spent by a business on non-current assets	All expenditure which is not capital expenditure. Costs associated with day-to-day running of business
Examples	Machinery, cars, computers	Materials, wages, power costs
Accounting treatment	Include on balance sheet as non-current asset	Include in income statement as expense

Cost centres and expenses

Definition

Allocation: process of allotting a whole item of overhead cost to a single cost centre.

For example: if the whole of the sales function is a single cost centre then sales commission paid to sales staff is allocated to sales cost centre

Definition

Apportionment: process of sharing out an overhead cost (on a suitable basis) to more than one cost centre.

For example: rent/rates may be apportioned on basis of floor area of building as this is likely to be the fairest method of spreading overheads over different cost centres

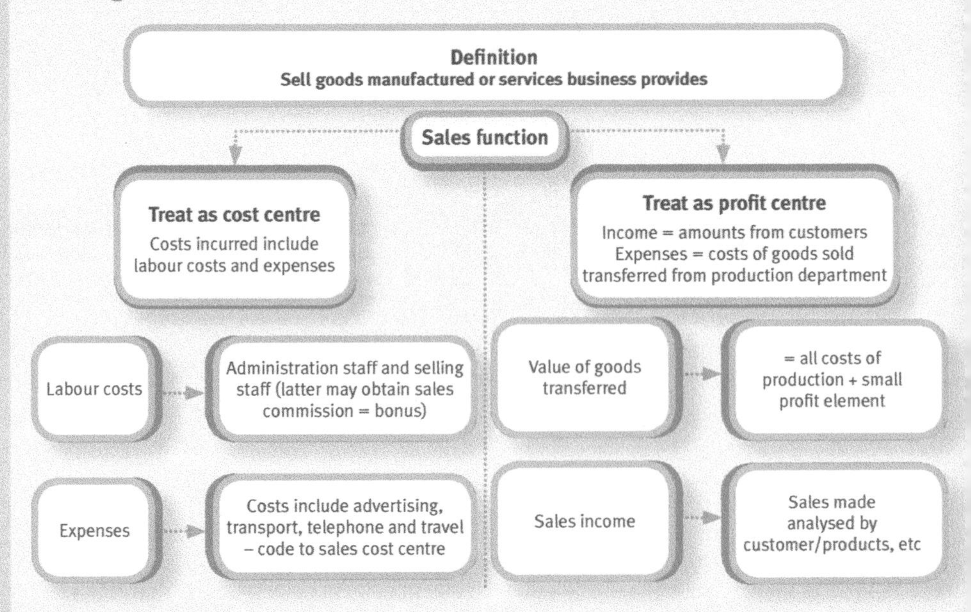
Selling function
Definition
Sell goods manufactured or services business provides
Sales function
Treat as cost centre
Costs incurred include labour costs and expenses
Treat as profit centre
Income = amounts from customers
Expenses = costs of goods sold transferred from production department
Labour costs
Administration staff and selling staff (latter may obtain sales commission = bonus)
Expenses
Costs include advertising, transport, telephone and travel – code to sales cost centre
Value of goods transferred
= all costs of production + small profit element
Sales income
Sales made analysed by customer/products, etc

Definition

Absorption of overheads:

Method of including fair proportion of the total overhead costs as part of the cost of each cost unit.

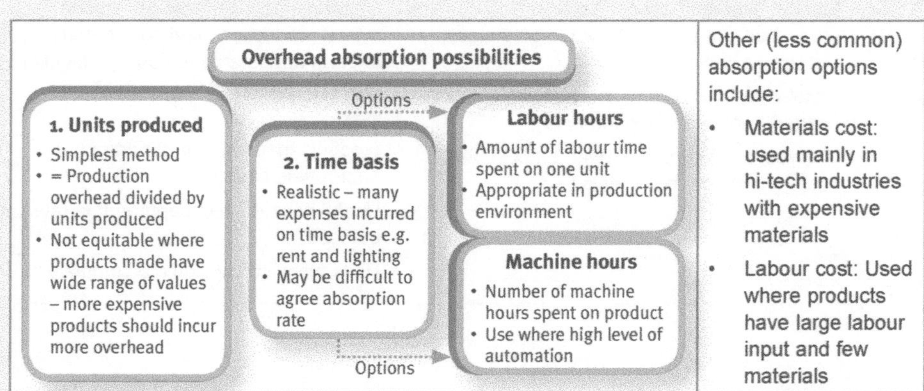

Other (less common) absorption options include:

- Materials cost: used mainly in hi-tech industries with expensive materials
- Labour cost: Used where products have large labour input and few materials

May also absorb based on prime cost.

Prime cost = total cost of direct materials, direct labour and any direct expenses.

Methods of overhead absorption

Two main absorption rates:

Blanket overhead absorption	Departmental overhead absorption
• Blanket overhead absorption = total production overheads absorbed on single absorption basis • Simple: no allocation of overheads needed to different departments • Unrealistic in that use of overheads in each department not considered	• Departmental overhead absorption = total production overhead for each department determined using allocation and apportionment • Total allocated overhead absorbed into products made in that department on appropriate basis • Useful because most appropriate rate can be used • Uses many calculations to complete

<table>
<tr>
<td>
Issue: Use of estimated overheads
<ul>
<li>Department absorption assumes cost of overhead known prior to absorption calculations taking place</li>
<li>Total costs not known until end of accounting period</li>
<li>Therefore use budgets to estimate amount of overhead</li>
<li>Budgeted overhead then apportioned to departments and absorbed into products</li>
<li>See example right</li>
</ul>
</td>
<td>
Example
<table>
<tr><td></td><td>Budget</td><td>Actual</td></tr>
<tr><td>Production overhead</td><td>$80,000</td><td>$85,000</td></tr>
<tr><td>Machine hours</td><td>20,000</td><td>21,000</td></tr>
</table>
Absorption rate = $80,000/20,000 = $4 machine hour
Production overhead absorbed =
<table>
<tr><td>$4 x 21,000 hours =</td><td>$84,000</td></tr>
<tr><td>Overhead incurred =</td><td>$85,000</td></tr>
<tr><td>Under-absorbed overhead =</td><td>$1,000</td></tr>
</table>
Under-absorbed overhead transferred to income statement (as a debit item)
</td>
</tr>
</table>

Non-production overheads can be allocated and absorbed in similar manner.

Exam focus

Don't get confused with allocation and apportionment. Costs are allocated to single cost centres and apportioned or 'shared out' between more than one cost centre.

chapter

8

Marginal and absorption costing

In this chapter

- Contribution.
- Absorption costing and marginal costing.
- Reconciliation of marginal and absorption costing profits.

Contribution

Definition

Contribution: sales value less all variable costs.

Selling price	$20
Direct materials	$6
Direct labour	$3
Variable overhead	$4
Fixed overhead	$20,000/month

Data for examples in this section

Selling price		$20
Direct materials	$6	
Direct labour	$3	
Variable overhead	$4	
		$13
Contribution per unit		$7

Assuming actual units produced = 20,000, then total contribution and profits are:

Total contribution	=	Sales units	x	contribution per unit	=	
		20,000	x	**$7**	=	**$140,000**
Less fixed costs						**$20,000**
Profit						**$120,000**

Absorption costing and marginal costing

	Absorption costing	Marginal costing
Definition	Cost accounting system that charges fixed and variable production overheads to cost units.	Cost accounting system where variable overheads are charged to cost units and fixed overheads to the income statement.
Inventory valuation	Includes variable and fixed overheads	Includes variable overheads only

In marginal costing

Assuming:

Budgeted production	20,000 units
Actual production	25,000 units
Production sold	22,000 units

- Inventory valued at marginal cost only
- Fixed costs written off in the accounting period to which they relate
- Production costs and closing inventory value simply the variable costs of production

Sales	22,000 x $20		$440,000
Variable costs			
Production costs	25,000 x $13	$325,000	
Less closing inventory	3,000 x $13	($39,000)	
			$286,000
Contribution			$154,000
Fixed costs			$20,000
Operating profit			$134,000

<table>
<tr>
<td>

In absorption costing

Assuming:

- Inventory valued includes fixed and variable costs
- Value therefore $13 from marginal costing plus $1/unit fixed costs ($20,000 cost with 20,000 units budgeted $14 per unit
- Over absorption of overhead credited to income statement
- Calculation is:

Fixed overhead absorbed (25,000 @$1)	$25,000
Fixed overhead incurred	$20,000
Over absorbed fixed overhead	$5,000

</td>
<td>

Sales	22,000 x $20		$440,000
Variable costs			
Production costs	25,000 x $14	$350,000	
Less closing inventory	3,000 x $14	($42,000)	
			$308,000
Operating margin			$132,000
Over-absorbed fixed overhead			$5,000
Operating profit			$137,000

</td>
</tr>
</table>

Reconciliation of marginal and absorption costing profits

• Only difference is inventory valuation • Value difference therefore relates to change in inventory units at difference in inventory valuation • In example, inventory units increased by 3,000 at $1 unit • Calculation right, show reconciliation	Operating profit – marginal costing	$134,000
	Operating profit – absorption costing	$137,000
	Difference	$3,000
	Increase in inventory level 3,000 units at $1/unit	$3,000

For absorption costing	Against absorption costing
• Gives correct financial statement inventory valuation (including fixed overheads) • Small business – shows profit expected on jobs • Under/over absorption fixed overhead analysis is useful for control	• Profit misleading because based on assumed activity level – would change with different levels • Inventory change distorts financial statements • Arbitrary apportionment of fixed overheads makes product comparisons difficult

chapter

9

Job, batch and process costing

In this chapter

- Specific order costing.
- Job costing.
- Batch costing.
- Process costing.
- Losses.
- Work-in-progress (WIP).

Specific order costing

There are two main types of costing system:

- **Specific order costing**, where the costs of distinct products or services are collected. Individual cost units are different according to individual customer's requirements. The main examples of specific order costing are job costing and batch costing.
- **Continuous costing**, where a series of similar products are produced. Costs are collected and averaged over the number of products or services produced to arrive at a cost per unit. The main examples of continuous costing are process costing and service costing which are considered in later chapters.

The cost units of different organisations will be of different types and this will tend to necessitate different costing systems.

The main types of cost unit are as follows:

Individual products designed and produced for individual customers	Groups of different products, possibly in different styles, sizes or colours, produced to be held in inventory until sold	Many units of identical products produced from a single production process. These units will be held in inventory until sold
Each individual product is a cost unit	Each batch is a cost unit	Each batch from the process is a cost unit
Job costing	**Batch costing**	**Process costing**

Job costing

Definition

A **job** is an individual product designed and produced as a single order for individual customers.

All of the actual costs incurred in a job are eventually recorded on a job cost card. A job cost card can take many forms but is likely at least to include the following information (see as follows):

<table>
<tr><th colspan="10">Job cost card</th></tr>
<tr><td colspan="5">Job number:</td><td colspan="5">Customer name:</td></tr>
<tr><td colspan="5">Estimate ref:</td><td colspan="5">Quoted estimate:</td></tr>
<tr><td colspan="5">Start date:</td><td colspan="5">Delivery date:</td></tr>
<tr><td colspan="5">Invoice number:</td><td colspan="5">Invoice amount:</td></tr>
<tr><th colspan="10">Costs</th></tr>
<tr><th colspan="5">Materials</th><th colspan="5">Labour</th></tr>
<tr><td>Date</td><td>Code</td><td>Qty</td><td>Price</td><td>$</td><td>Date</td><td>Grade</td><td>Hours</td><td>Rate</td><td>$</td></tr>
<tr><th colspan="5">Expenses</th><th colspan="5">Production overheads</th></tr>
<tr><td>Date</td><td>Code</td><td colspan="2">Description</td><td>$</td><td>Hours</td><td colspan="3">OAR</td><td>$</td></tr>
<tr><td></td><td></td><td colspan="2"></td><td></td><td></td><td colspan="3"></td><td></td></tr>
<tr><th colspan="10">Cost summary</th></tr>
<tr><td colspan="10">Direct materials</td></tr>
<tr><td colspan="10">Direct labour</td></tr>
<tr><td colspan="10">Direct expenses</td></tr>
<tr><td colspan="10">Production overheads</td></tr>
<tr><td colspan="10">Administrative overheads</td></tr>
<tr><td colspan="10">Selling and distribution overheads</td></tr>
<tr><td colspan="10">Total cost</td></tr>
<tr><td colspan="10">Invoice price</td></tr>
<tr><td colspan="10">Profit/loss</td></tr>
</table>

As well as recording the job costs on the job cost card they must also be recorded in the cost ledger accounts. Each job will have its own job ledger account to which the costs incurred are all debited.

Since each job is different, there will be no set price for each job. A customer often wants to be quoted a price for the job before the work begins, in which case the supplier might:

- estimate a fully-absorbed cost for the job
- add a profit mark-up to the cost, to arrive at a price to charge for the work.

In such cases, the organisation has to start by estimating the cost for the job and must decide what size the profit mark-up should be. Typically, the profit added on is a standard percentage of the total cost (a profit mark-up) or a standard percentage of sales price (a profit margin).

This form of pricing is known as cost-plus pricing.

Example

A job has production costs of $800. Administration overhead is added at 25% of production cost.

Full production cost =
$800 + (25% × $800) = $1,000.

- If profit **mark-up** is 20%

  Selling price =
  $1,000 + (20% × $1,000) = $1,200

- If profit **margin** is 20%

  Selling price = $\frac{\$1,000}{(100-20)\%} = \frac{\$1,000}{0.8} = \$1,250$

Batch costing

Definition

A **batch** is a group of identical but separately identifiable products that are all made together.

Each batch is very similar to a job and in exactly the same way as in job costing the costs of that batch are gathered together on some sort of batch cost card.

These costs will be the materials input into the batch, the labour worked on the batch, any direct expenses of the batch and the batch's share of overheads.

Cost of a cost unit

$$\text{Cost per unit} = \frac{\text{Total batch cost}}{\text{Number of units in batch}}$$

Process costing

Definition

Process costing is a method of costing used in industries including brewing, food processing, quarrying, paints, chemicals and textiles.

The cost per unit of finished output (X) is:

$$X = \frac{\text{Expected process costs}}{\text{Expected output units}}$$

- Process costs consist of direct materials, direct labour and production overheads.
- Costs of conversion, are the labour costs of the process plus the overheads of the process.
- When processing goes through several successive processes, the output from one process becomes an input direct material cost to the next process.
- Total costs therefore build up as the output goes through each successive processing stage.

The main problems with process costing are:

- how to treat losses
- how to value inventory and finished output when there are opening and closing inventories of work-in-process.

Exam focus

At this stage of your studies, you are only required to know how to value finished output and closing work-in-process when there is no opening work-in-process at the start of the accounting period.

Losses

In many processes, some losses in processing are inevitable. When losses occur, the problem arises as to how they should be accounted for.

If losses are a regular and expected aspect of the process then it is appropriate to calculate a cost per unit, based on the expected output from the process.

Example

If 100 units of material are input into a process with total costs incurred of $720 and it is expected that 10% will be lost, then the expectation is that 90 units will be produced at a cost of $720/90 = $8 per unit.

Any losses in excess of 10% would be treated as abnormal. If only 85 units were obtained from the process then the cost of the finished goods would be 85 × $8 = $680 and the abnormal loss would be 90 – 85 = 5 units × $8 = $40.

Definition

Normal loss is the expected amount of loss in a process. It is the level of loss or waste that management would expect to incur under normal operating conditions.

Valuation of normal loss

- If units of normal loss have no scrap value, their value or cost is nil.
- If units of normal loss have a scrap value, the value of this loss is its scrap value, which is set off against the cost of the process. In other words, the cost of finished output is reduced by the scrap value of the normal loss.

Work-in-progress (WIP)

At the end of a period, there could be unfinished production in process. Unfinished work-in-progress (or work-in-process) needs to be valued so that interim and periodic statements can be prepared.

Unfinished production is valued using the concept of '**equivalent units**'. Closing work-in-progress units are converted to 'equivalent units'. An equivalent unit, as the name might suggest, means the equivalent of one finished unit of output. If closing inventory of 100 units is 50% complete, it will be valued as 50 equivalent units.

In many processes, the direct materials are all input at the start of the process. If so, closing work-in-progress has all of its direct materials, and the units are unfinished only because the processing work has not yet been completed. In these situations, the valuation of output and closing inventory is separated into a valuation per unit for direct materials and a valuation per unit of conversion costs (direct labour and production overhead), each based on a different calculation of equivalent units.

Units of finished output count as one equivalent unit each.

The process account

The entries in the process account are summarised as follows:

Process a/c

	Units	$		Units	$
Direct material	X	X	Finished goods	X	X
Direct labour		X	Normal loss	X	X
Process overhead		X			
			Closing WIP	X	X
	X	X		X	X

chapter

10

Comparison of information and performance indicators

In this chapter

- Use of comparisons.
- Comparisons with budgets.
- Productivity measures.
- Performance measures and responsibility centres.

Use of comparisons

Comparisons made between current and historical and/or forecast data for purposes of management control.

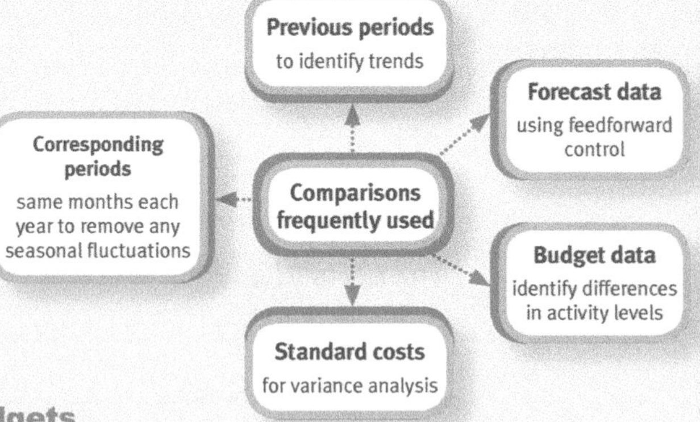

Comparisons with budgets

Expenses

- Flex the budget to actual activity level
- Budget for 8,000 units, actually produced 8,400 units
- Budget increased by 8,400/8,000 = 5%
- Example below, comparing actual expense to budget shows adverse variance of $2,580 ($30,580 – $28,000)
- Comparison to flexed budget shows adverse variance was less than this, $1,180

Expense	Budget $	Flexed budget $	Actual expense $	Variance $
Power	17,600	18,480	20,140	-1,660 A
Repairs	6,000	6,300	5,960	340 F
Packaging	4,400	4,620	4,480	140 F
Total	28,000	29,400	30,580	-1,180 A

Sales

Similar comparisons made.

Compare actual sales to budgeted sales (no flexing of budget).

Productivity measures

Definition

Productivity: measure relating goods or services produced to the resources used to produce them.

- Therefore attempt to produce maximum output from minimum inputs.

Note

- Production = quantity of goods or services produced.
- Productivity = measure of how efficiently those goods or services were produced.

Productivity ratios

Ratio	Calculation	Use
Production volume ratio	$\frac{\text{Actual output measured in standard hours}}{\text{Budgeted production hours}} \times 100\%$	Assesses overall production > 100% means production exceeds plan < 100% means production below plan
Capacity utilisation ratio	$\frac{\text{Actual hours worked}}{\text{Budgeted hours}} \times 100\%$	Indicates worker capacity > 100% means worked more than plan < 100% means worked less than plan
Efficiency ratio	$\frac{\text{Actual output measured in standard hours}}{\text{Actual hours worked}} \times 100\%$	Indicator of productivity > 100% indicates workers produced more per hour than expected < 100% indicates workers produced less per hour than expected

Capacity ratio = 90%, and Efficiency ratio = 127.8%, then Production volume ratio = 115% (90% x 127.8%)	Production volume ration = Capacity ratio x Efficiency ratio

Performance measures and responsibility centres

Manager performance measured against controllable costs only.

- Controllable cost = cost which manager can change e.g. number of workers
- Non-controllable cost = cost which manager cannot change e.g. factory rent

Cost centre performance	Profit centre performance	Investment centre performance
• Manager monitored according to costs incurred and resources utilised • Productivity ratios appropriate for measure of performance for production cost centre • Absolute cost incurred in cost centre useful control measure but cost per unit more informative	• Manager controls revenue and costs • Profit appropriate measure of performance • Use measures such as: – profit margin – cost to sales ratio – profit per unit	• Manager controls revenue, costs and level of investment • Efficiency of centre overall appropriate performance measure • Use measures such as ROCE and RI (see below)

Investment centre performance

Measure	Calculation	Use
Return on capital employed (ROCE)	$\frac{\text{Profit before interest and tax}}{\text{Capital employed}} \times 100\%$ Note: capital employed = non-current assets plus net current assets	Normally based on year-end capital. Used to compare performance of different divisions or same division year-on-year. Higher % indicates relatively less capital used to generate profit. Discourages investment because makes ratio appear worse e.g. falls.
Residual income (RI)	Investment centre profit – Notional interest on capital employed in centre	Includes only controllable costs, revenues and capital items. Shows residual income of centre – amount of profit over and above amount 'charged' for capital.

Data	ROCE	Residual income
Profit = \$55,800 Assets = \$329,000 Notional interest = 12%	$\frac{\$55,800}{\$329,000} \times 100\% = 17\%$	\$55,800 – 329,000 x 12% = \$16,320

Asset turnover ratio

- Measures how efficiently the assets of an organisation are used to generate revenue
- Calculated as follows:

$$\text{Asset turnover ratio} = \frac{\text{Revenue}}{\text{Capital employed}}$$

- Alternative calculation:

$$\text{Asset turnover} = \frac{\text{ROCE}}{\text{Profit margin}}$$

Exam focus

Examination questions may ask you to calculate the ratios in this section, or ask you to identify reasons for changes in those ratios. Check you can calculate the ratios but also understand why they may change.

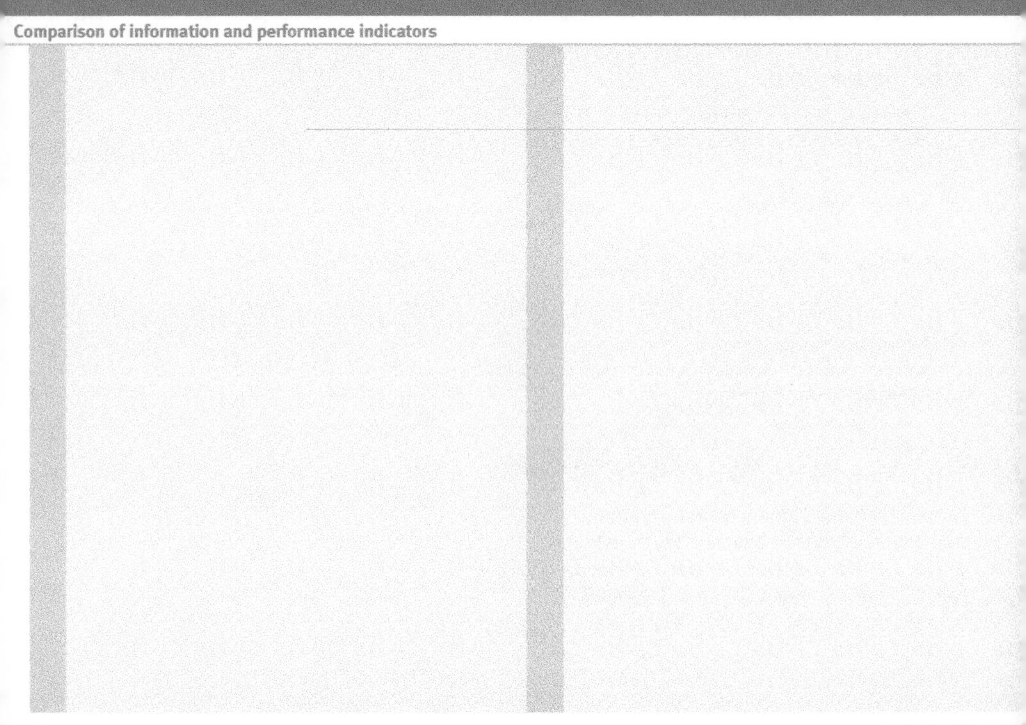

chapter

11

The spreadsheet system

In this chapter

- The use of spreadsheets.
- Benefits and limitations.
- Accessing a spreadsheet.
- Moving around the spreadsheet.
- Entering data.
- Formulae.
- Improving the spreadsheet's appearance.
- Spreadsheet errors.
- Spreadsheet security.
- Producing reports.
- Graphs and charts.
- Printing.

The use of spreadsheets

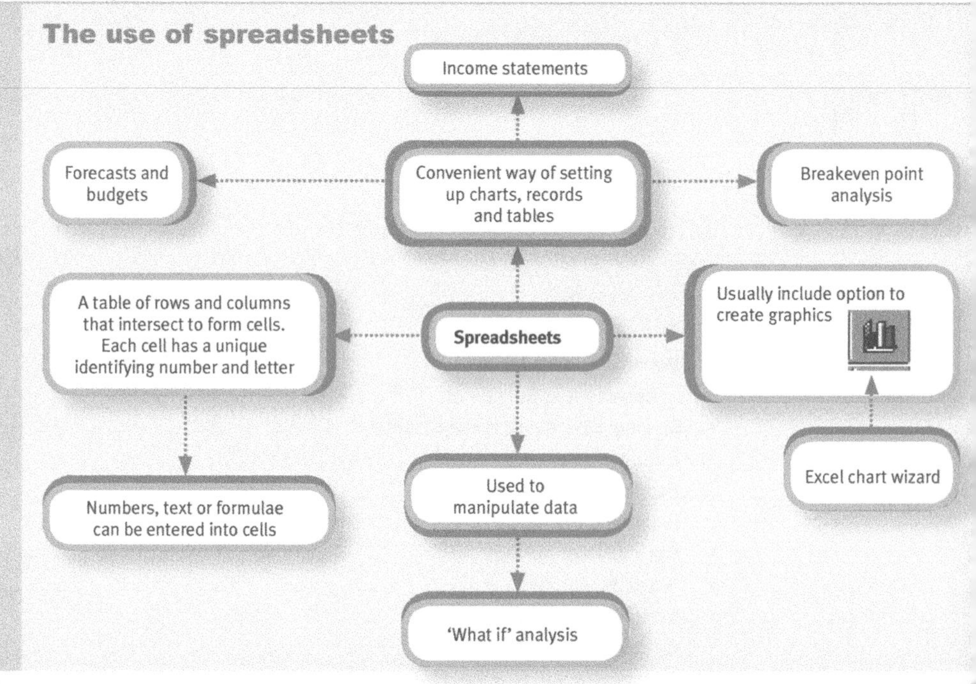

Benefits and limitations

Benefits	Limitations
• Can perform calculations automatically	• Can take time to develop
• Can cope with large quantities of data	• Data can be accidentally changed
• Useful for planning and control	• Poor inputs will lead to poor outputs
• Can be used for sensitivity analysis	• Development requires expertise
• Can create charts and graphs from data	• Should be secured

Accessing a spreadsheet

Running the program – Excel for windows

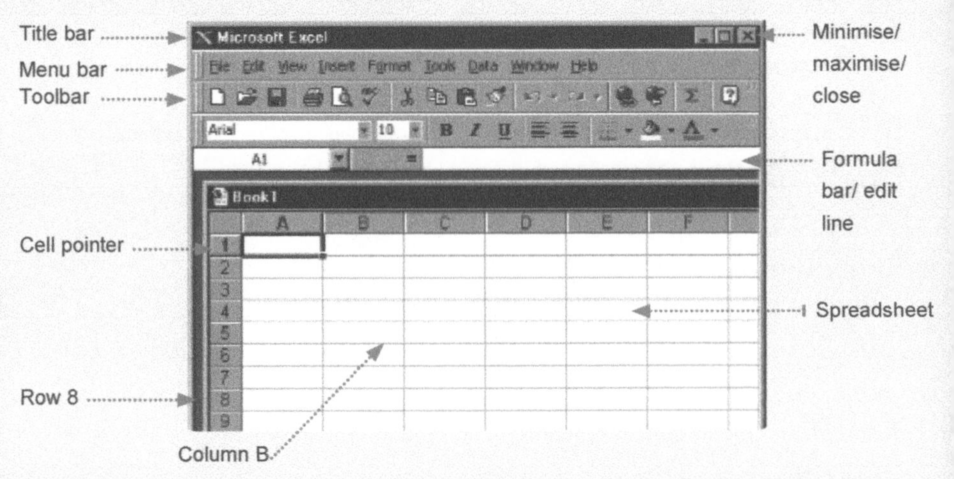

A **spreadsheet** is also known as a **worksheet**. A **workbook** is a collection of worksheets or spreadsheets.
(**Note**: your spreadsheet might be slightly different if you have another version of Excel.)

Moving around the spreadsheet

Moving around the spreadsheets

Cell pointer:

You can move around the spreadsheet by positioning the mouse pointer over the required cell and clicking on the cell to select it.

GOTO command:

In Excel key F5 is the GOTO key – by pressing the F5 key followed by the cell you require, the cell pointer will take you straight to the required cell.

Help facility:

Excel has a comprehensive help facility which provides both general help and context sensitive help:

Help button on menu bar

- Short cut key F1
- '?' on tool bar.

Entering data

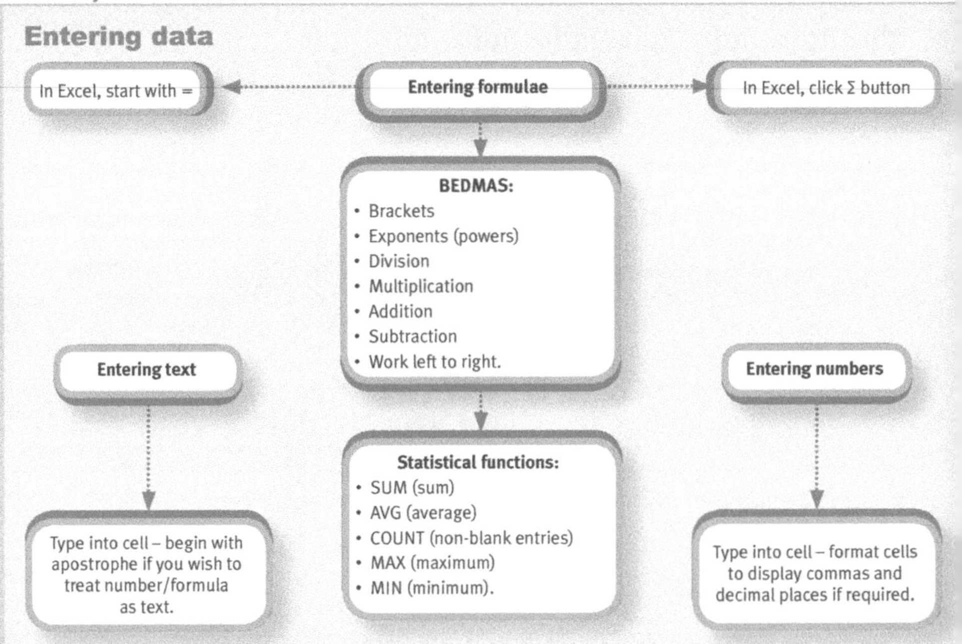

Formulae

To ensure that a formula refers to an **absolute** reference we have to put a $ sign before the column and/or row reference that we want to remain fixed.

Round function:

- Used to determine the number of decimal places to round to
- Syntax: =Round (number, digits)
- Use –1 as the digit to round to the nearest 10, –2 to the nearest 100 etc.

Present value function:

- Used to calculate the present value of an annuity
- Syntax: =PV(rate, number of periods, payment, date)
- Rate = the interest rate
- Number of periods = length of the annuity
- Payment = the cash flow amount
- Date = the start date (0 = today, 1 = 1 year's time etc.)

Net present value function

- Used to calculate the net present value of a series of cash flows
- Syntax: =NPV(rate, value1, value2, ...etc.)
- Rate = is the interest rate per period.
- Value 1 = is the first cashflow. It always assumes that this flow arrives at year 1
- Value 2 = is the second cashflow etc.
- This will give the present value of the future cash flows
- To get the overall NPV, the initial investment must be deducted

Internal Rate of Return function

- The will calculate the IRR of a stream of cash flows
- Syntax: =IRR(values, guess)
- For the formula to work an initial guess must be made at the IRR

The IF function

- Used to display one of two results depending on a previous set of data
- Syntax: =IF(logical test, value if true, value if false)

The ranking function

- Used to rank data
- Syntax: =Rank(Number, ref, order)
- Number = is the cell reference of the number to be ranked
- Ref = is the range of cells to use in ranking the Number
- Order = determines whether the Number is ranked in ascending or descending order. Type a "0" (zero) to rank in descending order (largest to smallest). Type a 1 to rank in ascending order (smallest to largest)

Improving the spreadsheet's appearance

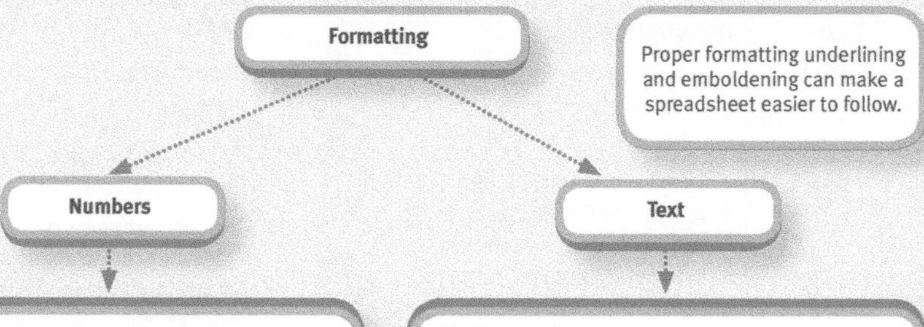

(1) Highlight numbers to be formatted.

(2) Click 'format' in menu bar.

(3) Select 'cells'.

(4) Select 'currency'.

(5) Select required format, e.g. £ to 2 decimal places.

(1) Change font.

(2) Put the titles in bold.

(3) Change column widths.

(4) Align column headings.

(5) Underline totals.

Spreadsheet errors

Error	Description
#DIV/0!	This occurs where we have tried to divide by zero or a blank cell
#NAME?	This occurs when we use a name that Excel doesn't recognise. This is common in incorrectly spelled function names
#REF!	This occurs when a formula uses an invalid cell reference
#VALUE!	This occurs when we attempt to use an incorrect data type

Spreadsheet security

Hiding rows/columns:

- Select the row (s) or column (s)
- Right click and choose the 'Hide' option
- To undo: choose the rows/columns either side, right click and choose the 'Unhide' option.

Password protection

- Access through the 'Save as' function
- Before saving click on the 'Tools' drop down menu
- Choose between password protecting access to the book, modifications or to display a warning to recommend read only access.

Protecting individual cells:

- Select the cells you do not want to protect
- Enter 'Format Cells' and in the 'Protection' tab untick the 'Locked' option
- Right click on the sheet name and choose to 'Protect sheet'
- Undo by right clicking the sheet and choosing 'Unprotect sheet'.

Producing reports

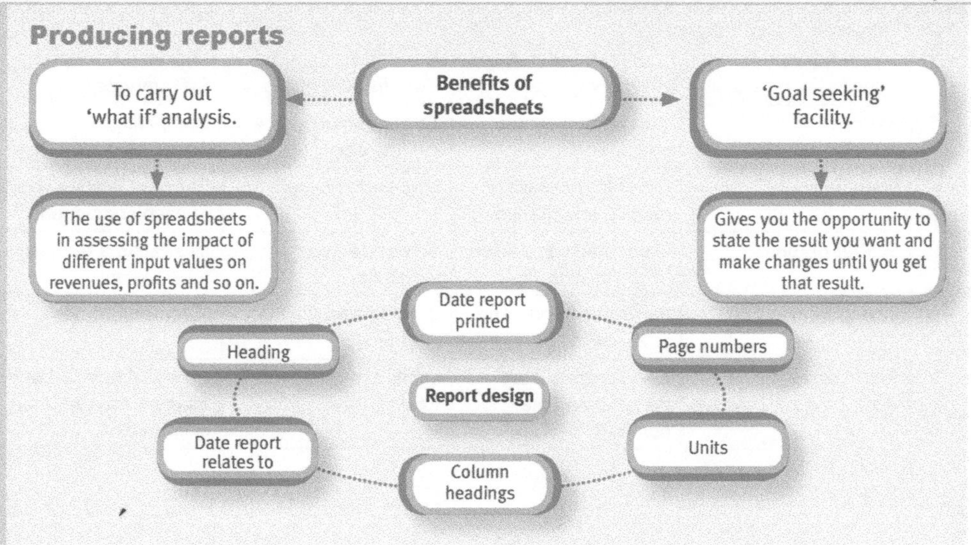

Graphs and charts

Type	Key advantage	Key disadvantage	Suitability
Bar/column	Can be broken into components	Totals and accuracy can be lost	Comparing components over time
Pie/doughnut	Good for assessing relative importance	May be too simple	Showing relative size of each component
Scatter graphs	Can cope with a wide range of data	Limited to two variables	Illustrating a random relationship
Line graphs	Illustrates trends and seasonality	Complicated if lines intersect	Identifying trends
Area chart	Can illustrate both the total and the components	Limited to one overall total	An alternative to bar charts when the total is important

Creating graphs

Steps:

1 Select data

2 Open the chart wizard

3 Choose chart type

4 Choose chart options

Chart options:

- Titles – to add titles to the chart or axes
- Legend – to determine where the key is displayed
- Data labels – to label bars/lines etc. on the chart
- Data table – to include the original data on the chart
- Axes – to remove an axes
- Gridlines – to remove gridlines

Printing

Users should examine the print preview (accessed from the print menu) before printing a spreadsheet. From this menu a user can change:

- Page setup – change the size of print and the type of paper to be used in the printer.
- Margins setup – choose how much blank border should surround the spreadsheet on a page.
- Header/footer settings – add headers and footers to act as titles for each print out. A user can also add page numbers if they choose to do so.
- Sheet setup – choose which part/area of the spreadsheet to print and whether to print the gridlines that normally appear in spreadsheets to separate cells. The user can also choose to repeat certain rows at the top of each page if the spreadsheet runs to more than one page.

Index

A

B

C

D

E

F

G

H

I

J

M